BACKYARD SCIENCE

BEAUTIFUL BIRDS

Harold Morris

TABLE OF CONTENTS

A Crabtree Seedlings Book

CRABTREE
Publishing Company
www.crabtreebooks.com

BIRDS

Birds live all over the world.

All birds have **feathers** and a **beak**.

Birds are all different colors and shapes.

Birds are all different sizes too!

bee hummingbird

The bee hummingbird is the smallest bird in the world. The ostrich is the biggest.

ostrich

Birds lay eggs.

Most birds build nests.

Most birds build
nests in the **spring**.

Nests can be built almost anywhere.

Some birds **migrate**.

same **area** all year.

All birds have wings.

But not all birds can fly.

Penguins cannot fly.
They use their wings to swim.

talons

Some birds have **talons**.

Some have webbed feet.

webbed feet →

Be a backyard scientist!

Study the birds in your backyard or in a park. Take notes. What shape and color are they? Are they building nests? What do you think they eat?

Glossary

area (AIR-ee-uh): An area is a part of a place, such as the southern part of a country.

beak (BEEK): A beak is the hard, sharp part of a bird's mouth.

feathers (FETH-urz): Feathers are the light, fluffy parts that cover a bird's body and wings.

migrate (MYE-grate): When birds migrate, they move from one area to another at a certain time of year, usually to move to warmer weather.

spring (SPRING): Spring is one of the four seasons: spring, summer, fall, and winter. Most birds lay eggs in the spring.

talons (TAL-uhnz): Talons are the sharp claws of a bird. Not all birds have talons.

Index

School-to-Home Support for Caregivers and Teachers

This book helps children grow by letting them practice reading. Here are a few guiding questions to help the reader build his or her comprehension skills. Possible answers appear here in red.

Before Reading

- **What do I think this book is about?** I think this book is about birds that live in backyards. I think this book is about what birds like to eat.

- **What do I want to learn about this topic?** I want to learn more about how birds fly. I want to learn where birds sleep at night.

During Reading

- **I wonder why...** I wonder why some birds don't fly. I wonder why birds have so many colorful feathers.

- **What have I learned so far?** I have learned that most birds build nests in the spring. I have learned that some birds have webbed feet.

After Reading

- **What details did I learn about this topic?** I have learned that all birds have beaks and feathers. I have learned that penguins cannot fly, and they use their wings to swim.

- **Read the book again and look for the glossary words.** I see the word *feathers* on page 5, and the word *talons* on page 18. The other glossary words are found on pages 22 and 23.

Library and Archives Canada Cataloguing in Publication

CIP available at Library and Archives Canada

Library of Congress Cataloging-in-Publication Data

CIP available at Library of Congress

Crabtree Publishing Company

www.crabtreebooks.com   1–800–387–7650

Written by: Harold Morris

Production coordinator and Prepress technician: Tammy McGarr

Print coordinator: Katherine Berti

Print book version produced jointly with Blue Door Education in 2022

Printed in the U.S.A./CG20210915/012022

PHOTO CREDITS:
istock.com, shutterstock.com, COVER: VP Photo Studio, Kletr, sign art on cover and title page © ecco. PG2-3; eurotravel. PG4-5; Jillian Cain Photography, bookguy, xtrekx. PG6-7; GlobalP, blewulis, JessicaHandPhotography, Flatcoater, fusaromike, moose henderson, Photitos2016, MichaelStubblefield. PG8-9; Photitos2016, Aaron Amat, undefined undefined, Koraysa. PG10-11; DrPAS, Ievgenii Meyer , v_zaitsev. PG12-13; Gigi001, liveslow, SteveByland, nameinfame, Tinieder, JJFORBES46044. PG14-15; TT, Dee Carpenter Photography. PG16-17; vladsilve, katsuramiyamoto. Pg18-19; B_Seaman, bazilfoto, amwu. Pg20-21; Craig Lopetz, Gary Kavanagh. PG22-23; KEMSAB.. PG24; Mexitographer

Published in the United States
Crabtree Publishing
347 Fifth Ave.
Suite 1402-145
New York, NY 10016

Published in Canada
Crabtree Publishing
616 Welland Ave.
St. Catharines, Ontario
L2M 5V6